Diverse and Different

LEVEL 7
/i/

Teaching Tips

Turquoise Level 7
This book focuses on the grapheme /i/.

Before Reading
- Discuss the title. Ask readers what they think the book will be about. Have them support their answer.
- Ask readers to sort the words on page 3. Read the words together. Reinforce that /i/ can have a short /i/ sound or a long /i/ sound.

Read the Book
- Encourage readers to read independently, either aloud or silently to themselves.
- Prompt readers to break down unfamiliar words into units of sound and string the sounds together to form the words. Then, ask them to look for context clues to see if they can figure out what these words mean. Discuss new vocabulary to confirm meaning.
- Urge readers to point out when the focused phonics grapheme appears in the text. Does it have a short /i/ sound or a long /i/ sound?

After Reading
- Ask readers comprehension questions about the book. How were people in the book different? How did they respect one another?
- Encourage readers to think of other words with the /i/ grapheme. On a separate sheet of paper, have them write the words into two columns: one under the short /i/ sound and the other under the long /i/ sound.

© 2024 Booklife Publishing
This edition is published by arrangement with Booklife Publishing.

North American adaptations © 2024 Jump!
5357 Penn Avenue South
Minneapolis, MN 55419
www.jumplibrary.com

Decodables by Jump! are published by Jump! Library.
All rights reserved. No part of this book may be reproduced in any form without written permission from the publisher.

Library of Congress Cataloging-in-Publication Data is available at www.loc.gov or upon request from the publisher.

ISBN: 979-8-88996-870-2 (hardcover)
ISBN: 979-8-88996-871-9 (paperback)
ISBN: 979-8-88996-872-6 (ebook)

Photo Credits
Images are courtesy of Shutterstock.com. With thanks to Getty Images, Thinkstock Photo and iStockphoto. Cover – Master1305, AnnGaysorn, Inside Creative House. 4–5 – CREATISTA, wavebreakmedia. 6–7 – pixdeluxe, Pranay Chandra Singh. 8–9 – Ermolaev Alexander, kdshutterman, Luc Pouliot. 10–11 – Ilike, Jure Divich. 12–13 – Lorena Fernandez, Freeograph, Irina Starikova3432. 14–15 – Irina Starikova3432, Veronica Louro. 16 – Shutterstock.

Can you sort these words into two groups? One group has **i** as in **pig**. One group has **i** as in **mind**.

picnic

wild

bring

child

kind

stick

find

mint

Are you the same as the adults at home? What about the class you are in? Is each child the same? No! We are all different.

In this class, Si is different from Tim. Tim is different from Rich. Rich is different from Ida. Ida is different from Idris. The list goes on!

The important thing to remember is that we must be kind to all people. We are all different, and that is fantastic!

Our minds all work in different ways. If I find that I am good at one thing, you might find that you are good at a different thing.

Mike likes to go into the wild in his free time. He sees which animals he can find in the woods on trips with his sister.

Look, a spider!

Irene prefers to spend her free time reading in a silent room. It is important for Irene to have some quiet time. Loud noises can make her feel stressed.

On Fridays, Irene and Mike find a quiet room and chat. Mike tells Irene about the animals he found. Irene tells Mike what she has been reading. They are good friends.

Ivan is best pals with Eli. Eli is blind, which means his sight is different from Ivan's. Eli and Ivan spend all week thinking of quizzes.

In class on Friday, they see who wins. Eric wins. He is a whiz and amazing at quizzes!

Isaac helps his elders. He likes to listen to Lorna's tales. She cannot do it now, but she was a pilot in the past.

Speaking to people like Lorna helps Isaac to not form ideas about people based on what they look like. People can surprise you!

It is not just fine to be different. It is amazing to be different! We must all be kind and remember that we are all amazing, no matter what!

Say the name of each object below. Is the "i" in each a short /i/ sound or a long /i/ sound?